NATIONAL GEOGRAPHIC

What Will Happen Today?

Corey David

I wonder what will happen today?
Am I likely to see a flying fish?

Or am I more likely to see a soaring bird?

Am I likely to hold a furry monkey?

Or am I more likely to hold a fuzzy cat?

5

Am I likely to climb a tall mountain?

Or am I more likely to climb a small tree?

7

Am I likely to hear a growling lion?

Or am I more likely to hear a barking dog?

Am I likely to ride in an airplane?

Or am I more likely to ride in Mom's car?